National Curricul...

**Key Stage 1
Age 6–7 years**

PRACTICE PAPERS
KEY STAGE 1
National Tests
MATHS

1999 edition

First published 1997
Reprinted 1997
Revised 1997, 1998
Reprinted 1999

Letts Educational
Aldine House
Aldine Place
London W12 8AW
Telephone: 0181-740 2266
e-mail: mail@lettsed.co.uk
website: http://www.lettsed.co.uk

Text: © BPP (Letts Educational) Ltd 1998
Author: Sarah Carvill
The publishers gratefully acknowledge Judith Morris and Jan Pickering for their contributions.

Prepared by *specialist* publishing services, Milton Keynes

Design and illustrations:
© BPP (Letts Educational) Ltd 1998
Page layout and illustrations: Tim Lole
Original page design by
Ian Foulis Associates, Saltash

All Rights Reserved. No part of this publication may be reproduced, stored in a retrieval system, or transmitted, in any form or by any means, electronic, mechanical, photocopying, recording or otherwise, without the prior permission of Letts Educational.

British Library Cataloguing in Publication Data
A CIP record for this book is available from the British Library.
ISBN 1 85758 807 X
Printed in Great Britain by Sterling Press, Wellingborough
Letts Educational is the trading name of
BPP (Letts Educational) Ltd

CONTENTS

Introduction	2
What you need to know about the National Tests	3
Preparing and practising for the National Tests	5
Test A	
Questions 1–35 (Levels 2–3)	7
Test B	
Questions 1–35 (Levels 2–3)	19
Test C	
Questions 1–12 (Extension paper, Level 4)	31
Answers and notes to parents – Test A	38
Answers and notes to parents – Test B	44
Answers and notes to parents – Test C	49
Finding your child's level	53
How to mark the questions	54
Marking grids	54

INTRODUCTION

YOUR CHILD AND KEY STAGE 1 NATIONAL TESTS

All pupils in Year 2 (ages 6 to 7) will take National Tests and Tasks in English and Mathematics. These important tests are designed to be an objective assessment of the work your child will have done during Key Stage 1 of the National Curriculum.

Pupils will also have their school work assessed by their teachers. The assessments will be set alongside your child's results in the National Tests to give a clear picture of his or her overall achievement.

The tasks will be carried out between January and June 1999 and the tests will take place in May 1999.

The results of your child's tests and tasks, together with the teacher assessments, will be reported to you in July.

HOW THIS BOOK WILL HELP YOUR CHILD

There is plenty of practice in the types of questions children will face in the Key Stage 1 National Tests for Mathematics.

The author provides answers and a marking scheme to allow you to check how your child has done.

Using the information in 'Notes to parents' you can help your child with questions which are answered incorrectly and advise on how to improve his or her answers.

There is a marking grid to record your child's results and help you estimate the level of the National Curriculum within which your child is working.

WHAT YOU NEED TO KNOW ABOUT THE NATIONAL TESTS

KEY STAGE 1 TESTS – HOW THEY WORK

Between the ages of five and seven (Years 1–2) children cover Key Stage 1 of the National Curriculum. From January to June of Year 2, in the final year of Key Stage 1, they are given tasks (practical activities) and tests (commonly known as SATs) in English and Mathematics. The tasks and tests are carried out under the supervision of teachers in school. They are also marked by teachers. The results are then brought together for comparison by external moderators.

Progress in Science, on the other hand, is based on children's performance throughout Key Stage 1 according to teacher assessment.

The tasks and tests in English and Mathematics help to find out what the children have learned. They also help parents and teachers to know whether the children are reaching the national standards set out in the National Curriculum.

The tasks and tests will provide a brief summary in Year 2 of your child's attainment in specific aspects of Mathematics, whilst teacher assessment is based on the full range of his or her work in relation to the Programmes of Study (the detail of what pupils should be taught for each Key Stage).

When the school has the final collated results of the children's tasks and tests, the results are reported to you as parents by the end of July in the same year. Together with those results, you will receive the results of classroom assessments made by the teachers, based on the work your child has done during the school year. In addition, you will be given a summary of the overall results for the other children in the school, and for children nationally. This will help you to know how your child is doing compared with other children of the same age.

The school's report will explain to you what the results show about your child's progress, strengths and particular achievements and will suggest targets for development. It will also explain how to follow up the results with the teachers and why the task and test results may differ from their assessment.

WHY THE KEY STAGE 1 TASKS AND TESTS ARE IMPORTANT

Naturally, it is important that children do as well as they can in their National Tasks and Tests. For although the results are not used to determine what class your child will move up to in Key Stage 2, they inevitably provide the next teacher with a picture of your child's overall attainment.

LEVELS OF ATTAINMENT: KNOWING HOW WELL YOUR CHILD IS DOING

The National Curriculum divides each subject into a number of levels, from 1 to 8. On average, children are expected to advance one level for every two years they are at school. It is reasonable to expect that by the end of Key Stage 1, most children should be between Levels 1 and 3, Level 2 being the level which the majority is expected to reach. On very rare occasions, a child at the end of Key Stage 1 may achieve Level 4. This should be recognised as an exceptional result. The table overleaf includes the levels for 7 to 11 year-olds to give you an overall picture of how your child should progress.

WHAT YOU NEED TO KNOW ABOUT THE NATIONAL TESTS

		7 years	11 years
■ Exceptional performance	Level 6		■
	Level 5		■
■ Exceeded targets for age group	Level 4	■	■
■ Achieved targets for age group	Level 3	■	■
	Level 2	■	■
□ Working towards targets for age group	Level 1	■	■

YOUR CHILD COMPARED WITH HIS OR HER OWN AGE GROUP

There are different Key Stage 1 National Tasks and Tests for different attainment levels. This is to ensure that pupils can be set a task or test in which they are able to show positive achievement, and are not discouraged by having to answer questions which are either too easy or too difficult.

Most children will take one paper for Levels 2 to 3 in Mathematics including oral questions. The paper will take about 45 minutes. Exceptional pupils may be entered for the Key Stage 2 tests to give them the chance to achieve a Level 4.

This book concentrates on Levels 2 and 3, giving plenty of practice to help children achieve the best level possible. There are also some higher level questions for very able pupils. Do not worry if your child cannot do these questions. If he or she can reach Level 3 having done the main questions, then your child will already be above the majority of children of his or her age. The table below shows you what percentage of pupils, nationally, reached each of the levels in the 1997 test for Mathematics at Key Stage 1.

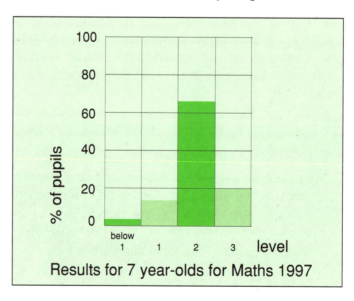

Results for 7 year-olds for Maths 1997

PREPARING AND PRACTISING FOR THE NATIONAL TESTS

MATHS AT KEY STAGE 1

The questions in this book will help you prepare your child by testing him or her on the Key Stage 1 curriculum for Mathematics. For assessment purposes, the current National Curriculum divides Mathematics into three sections, called Attainment Targets (ATs). The first AT, Using and Applying Mathematics, is assessed only by the teacher in the classroom, not in the written tests, although children will be applying and using mathematical knowledge and understanding in answering the test questions. The other two ATs are:

AT2 Number

AT3 Shape, Space and Measure

The Mathematics National Curriculum defines the level descriptions for each of the three ATs. These are taken together to give an overall level for Mathematics. The test papers have questions covering ATs 2 and 3.

USING THIS BOOK TO HELP YOUR CHILD PREPARE FOR THE NATIONAL TEST IN MATHS

This book contains four basic features :

Questions:
two test papers for Levels 2 to 3, and one extension paper for Level 4 (note that this differs from what happens in the National Tests where an exceptional child will be entered for the Key Stage 2 Test)

Answers:
showing acceptable responses and marks

Notes to parents:
giving advice to help improve your child's score and ensure that common mistakes are avoided

Level chart:
showing you how to interpret your child's marks to arrive at a level

Details of how to run the tests at home are given on the next page. Information about how to mark the tests and assess your child can be found at the end of the tests.

In the margin of each question page there are several small boxes (one for each question), each divided in half, with the mark available for that question at the bottom and a blank at the top for you to fill in your child's score.

PREPARING AND PRACTISING FOR THE NATIONAL TESTS

SIMULATING TEST CONDITIONS

Allow as much time as your child requires for each of the Levels 2 to 3 tests. Most children demonstrate what they can do in about 45 minutes. Allow your child to carry out the tests in a place where he or she is comfortable and to do them on separate occasions.

Tell your child:

- that you will start each of Tests A and B by reading out five questions while he or she writes down the answers.
- to read each question, work out the answer and then write it in the space provided. Where no answer box is given the answer should be written anywhere on the appropriate section of the page (except in the boxes provided for marking).
- that he or she can have as much help as necessary when reading words in questions, but no help with reading numbers or working out answers.
- that he or she can use number apparatus from the following: counters, number lines, cubes in ones and tens or other structural material using blocks, rods or abaci.
- that he or she can use a centimetre ruler with which he or she is familiar.
- that he or she can use a mirror for any symmetry questions.
- that there is plenty of space he or she can use for working out, writing or drawing answers either in the book or on separate sheets of paper.
- to use the working out sheets provided on pages 28 and 36.
- to change his or her answer by rubbing or crossing it out, if he or she makes a mistake.
- that some questions are harder than others; that if he or she cannot do one question then it is fine to go on to the next one which might be easier and go back to difficult ones later.
- that some of the questions have pictures which may help to work out the answers.
- that he or she can take as long as necessary to finish the questions.
- that when he or she has finished the answers can be checked.

MARKING THE QUESTIONS

Guidance on marking is given at the end of the tests section (see page 52).

FINALLY, AS THE TESTS DRAW NEAR

As the testing season approaches make sure your child is as relaxed and confident as possible. You can help by encouraging your child to believe in him or herself and the teacher! Remind your child of the need to concentrate, but to minimise tension encourage him or her to enjoy these tests. Remember, at this stage most children won't know they are sitting formal tests.

Look out for signs of anxiety. Although many children look forward to tests it is only natural that some may be nervous if they are aware that the tests are approaching. Reassure your child that though these tests are important they are not the only means by which he or she will be assessed.

TEST A: LEVELS 2–3

MATHS

Read out these instructions carefully to your child. Explain that he or she should listen to you and then show the answer on the next page.

TEST A

1. What is 5 less than 8?
   Write your answer in box a.

2. There are 8 girls and 6 boys on the playground.
   How many children are there altogether?
   Write your answer in box b.

3. Write the number 47 in box c.

4. Andrew has 2 boxes with 6 eggs in each box.
   How many eggs does he have altogether?
   Look at box d.
   Which of these would you use to work out the answer to the question?
   Now I'll read the question again.
   (Repeat question and add…)
   Put a ring round the one that will give the right answer.

5. Look at the clocks.
   Put a tick beside the clock that shows a quarter past three.

Now continue with the paper.

TEST A: LEVELS 2–3

1

[ ] a

2

[ ] b

3

[ ] c

4

| 6 + 2   6 − 2   2 × 6   2 + 2 |

d

5

 [ ]

 [ ]

 [ ]

 [ ]

TEST A: LEVELS 2–3

6 Write in the missing numbers.

7 Draw a ring round the odd numbers.

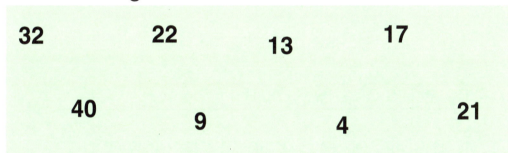

Use the number line for questions 8, 9, 10 and 11.

8 24 + 13 = ...

9 42 − 9 = ...

10 How many more is 41 than 27? ....

11 24 + 9 = ...

TEST A: LEVELS 2–3

This block graph shows how many children like cherryade, lemonade, cola and orange.

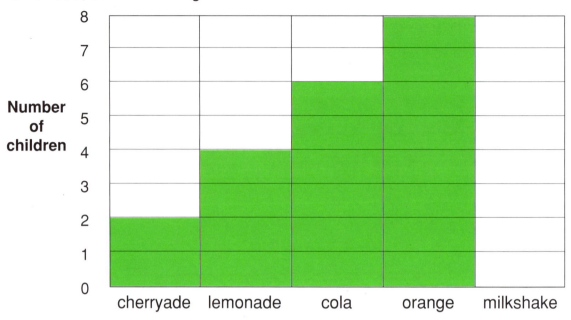

12 Five children like milkshake best.

Show this on the graph.

13 More children like orange than lemonade.

How many more? ....

14 Colour $\frac{1}{4}$ of these cakes.

15 Colour $\frac{1}{2}$ of this circle.

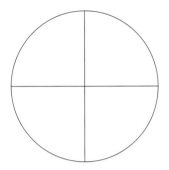

16 Find 2 shapes on the case with only 4 straight sides.
Draw a ring round each one.

TEST A: LEVELS 2–3

17 Josie has these coins.

How much money has she altogether? .... p

18 Write the missing number to complete these sums.

5 + 4 = ...   8 + ... = 12

.... + 11 = 15

19 Write these numbers in order, starting with the smallest.

35   2   97   152   14   79

....

20   38 + 29 = ...

21   Twelve children want to go on a lake.

There are 3 boats and an equal number of children get into each boat.

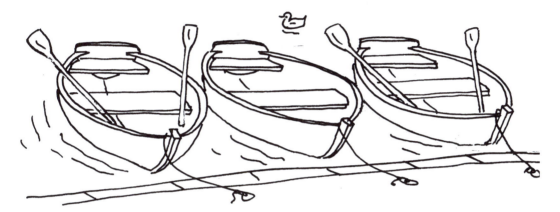

How many children get into each boat? ....

22   The clock shows the time a cartoon started.

It started at 3:40 p.m.
It lasted for 15 minutes.

Write the time the cartoon finished on the clock.

TEST A: LEVELS 2–3

23 This ladybird has 10 spots.

How many spots altogether have 7 ladybirds? ....

24 88 – 32 = ...

25 Tick the shapes which have reflective symmetry.

26 Some of these numbers can be divided exactly by 10.

15   30   45   18   37   90   49

Draw a circle round each number which can be divided exactly by 10.

14

27 5 ice creams cost £1.00 altogether.

How much does each ice cream cost? ....

28 Measure these with your ruler.

The crayon is .... cm long.

The pencil is .... cm long.

29 The pencil is .... cm longer than the crayon.

TEST A:
LEVELS 2–3

30  This is a cuboid.

A cuboid has

.... faces

.... corners

31  This is a cylinder.

A cylinder has

.... faces

32 Paul and Samantha went to the Fun Fair.
Here are their tickets.

How much did it cost for the 2 children? ....

33 Fill in the missing numbers to finish the pattern.

   4   8   12   ....

34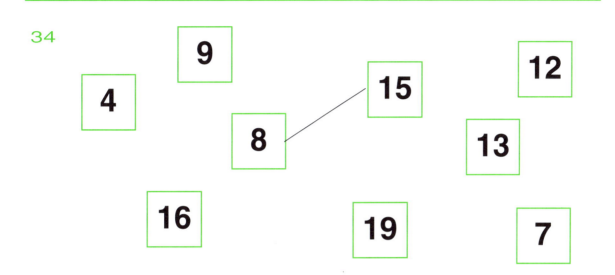

The 2 numbers joined together have a difference of 7.

Join 2 other numbers together that have a difference of 7.

35   This shape has one right angle.

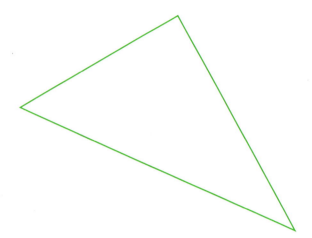

Draw a shape which has 4 right angles.

TEST B: LEVELS 2–3

Read out these instructions carefully to your child. Explain that he or she should listen to you and then show the answer on the next page.

TEST B

1. How many fives in 25?
   Write your answer in box a.

2. Draw round the coins that make 23p

3. What is 15 subtract 9?
   Write your answer in box b.

4. Think of an odd number between 2 and 8.
   Write your answer in box c.

5. One of these shapes is a cylinder.
   Put a ring round the cylinder.

**TEST B:
LEVELS 2–3**

1  a

2

3  b

4   c

5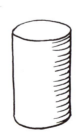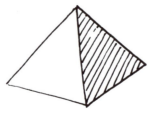
 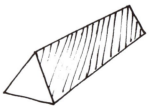

20

TEST B: LEVELS 2–3

6 Use two of these number cards to make 15.

.... + ... = 15

7 Now make 15 using 2 other cards.

.... + ... = 15

8 The numbers in the triangles make a pattern.
   Fill in the missing numbers.

   △2 + △9 = △11

   △12 + △9 = △21

   △22 + △9 = △31

   △ + △ = △

   △ + △ = △

9   Write the missing numbers in these balls.

10 Circle the even numbers.

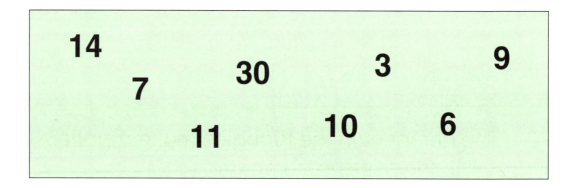

11 Measure this line.

_____ .... cm

12 Now draw a line 5cm longer than this line.

13 Add 14 to 11.

TEST B: LEVELS 2–3

14 Draw round the coins needed to buy an orange.

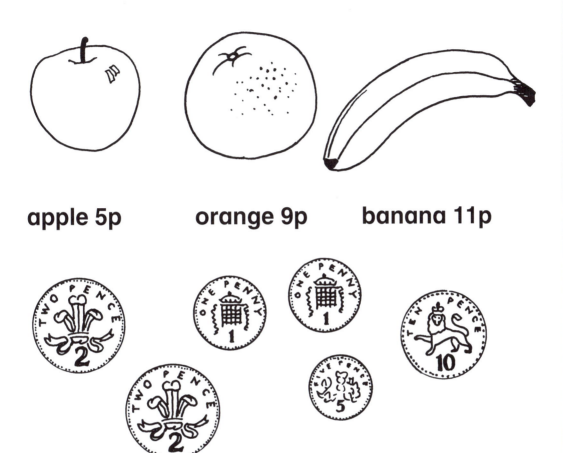

apple 5p **orange 9p** **banana 11p**

15 Write the numbers in order.

```
    20        9        23
         3
                    17
      8        14
```

Start with the greatest number.

....

The children collected stickers.

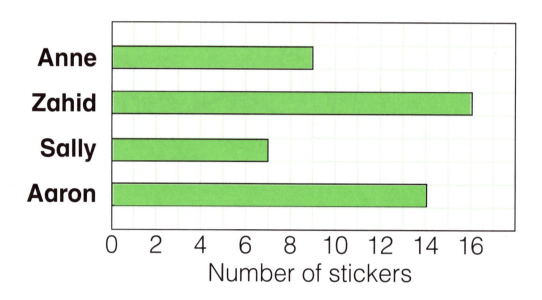

16 Who collected the most stickers? ....

17 How many stickers did Anne collect? ....

18 How many stickers were collected by the children altogether? ....

19 Write the time in numbers and words.

.... : ....

....

20 What time would it be half an hour later?

....

TEST B: LEVELS 2–3

What fraction of each shape is shaded?

21 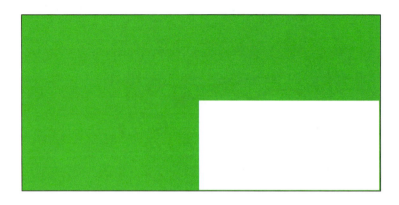 ....

22 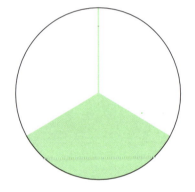 ....

23   39 + 47 = ...

24   There are 33 children in Class 2 and 29 children in Class 3.

How many more children are in Class 2 than in Class 3? ....

25   62 − 24 = ...

26 There are 24 sweets in a tube.

A quarter of the sweets are red.

How many sweets are red ? ....

Complete the patterns.

27

28

29 Sort these numbers to the nearest 10.

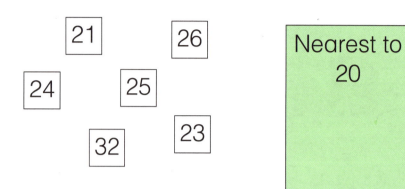

Nearest to 20	Nearest to 30

30 Helen travelled by bus one afternoon.

She started her journey at this time.   She finished her journey at this time.

How long was her journey?

TEST B: LEVELS 2–3

31 Draw two lines of symmetry on this shape.

32 Use two of these number cards

and this sign −

to make 19.

  = 19

TEST B: LEVELS 2–3

33 Draw round the shapes that have 4 right angles.

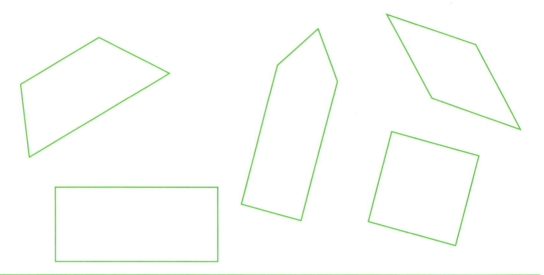

	Chairs	Tables
Class 1	19	10
Class 2	28	12
Class 3	24	11
Class 4	33	17
Class 5	29	16
Class 6	31	15

In a school the number of chairs and tables were counted in each class.

34 Which class has most chairs? ....

How many more tables are in Class 5 than in Class 3? ....

35 How many classes have more chairs than Class 2? ....

TEST C: LEVEL 4
EXTENSION PAPER

1   The children bring different amounts of money to the school tuck shop.

Mai Ling 83p   Tom 79p   Chloe 95p   Josh 62p

a   How much do Tom and Chloe have altogether ?

....

b   How much do Josh and Mai Ling have altogether ?

....

c   How much do Chloe and Josh have altogether ?

....

Note: this question continues on the next page.

2   How much more has

a   Tom than Josh ? ....

b   Chloe than Mai Ling ? ....

c   Mai Ling than Tom ? ....

3   Tom bought a bar of chocolate for 23p and 3 lollies for 4p each.

How much money did he have left ? ....

TEST C: LEVEL 4 EXTENSION

4   On one day in a car park there are

37	black cars
9	motorbikes
105	red cars
14	vans
3	coaches
90	blue cars

Put the totals of each kind of vehicle in order, starting with the one with the largest total.

....

5   How many vehicles are there altogether? ....

6   There are exactly 10 times as many ....

    as ....

Note: this question continues on the next page.

7 How much money is paid to the car park on this day?

....

8 427 − 165 = ...

9 Measure the perimeters of these shapes.

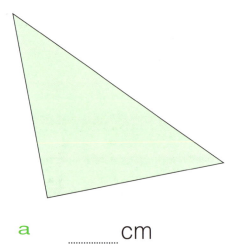

a .... cm   b .... cm

10   A film was showing at the cinema.
     This clock shows when the film started.

_____ p.m.

This clock shows when the film finished.

_____ p.m.

How long did the film last? _____

TEST C: LEVEL 4 EXTENSION

11 A survey was made of pets owned by children in Class 7B.

There are 30 children in the class.

40% of the class have no pets.

So 12 children have no pets.

a 20% of the class own a dog.

How many children is this ? ....

b 10% of the class own a cat.

How many children is this ? ....

c $\frac{1}{5}$ of the class own a hamster.

How many children is this ? ....

d Three children own a fish.

What fraction of the class is this ? ....

Note: this question continues on the next page.

TEST C: LEVEL 4 EXTENSION

e   Write in the table the number of children who have each pet, or who have no pets.

	dogs
	hamsters
	cats
	fish
	no pets

12 Now draw a bar chart to show the information. Label the sides and give it a title.

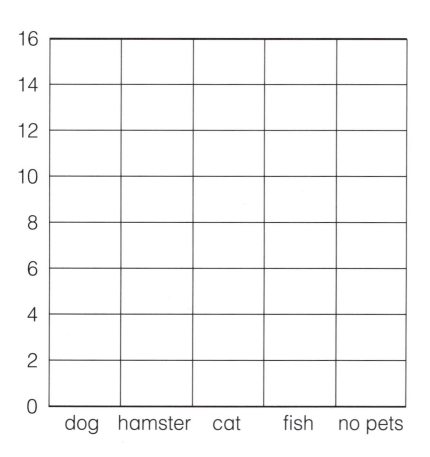

ANSWERS: TEST A

TEST A

1 **3** 1 mark

> **Note to parents**
> This question aims to encourage your child to subtract mentally whilst recognising the wording 'less than' as a subtraction operation.

2 **14** 1 mark

> **Note to parents**
> Quick mental recall of addition facts to 20 will assist your child when solving a variety of problems in mathematics.

3 **47** 1 mark

> **Note to parents**
> Children need to be able to place digits in the correct order when writing numbers up to 99.

4 **2 x 6** 1 mark

> **Note to parents**
> Children need to be able to identify the operations they use when performing calculations mentally.

5  1 mark

> **Note to parents**
> Children must recognise positioning of hands on a clock face for quarter to, quarter past and o'clock

6 12, 13, **14**, 15, **16**, **17**. 1 mark

All three numbers must be filled in to gain mark.

> **Note to parents**
> This question aims to encourage your child to explore numbers from 1 to 20. It involves ordering numbers in correct sequence, adding on 1, and knowing which number precedes or follows another.

ANSWERS: TEST A

7 **9, 13, 17, 21.** 1 mark
All four numbers must be circled to gain mark.

> **Note to parents**
> Odd numbers are those which do not form pairs exactly. They will end with 1,3,5,7 or 9.

8 **37** 1 mark

9 **33** 1 mark

10 **14** 1 mark

> **Note to parents**
> Number lines, from 0 to 100 (marked off in units), are a useful tool for children to count on or back when carrying out addition and subtraction and to help understanding of place value and the number system.
> e.g. 24 + 13 = 37
>
> 23 24 25 26 27 28 29 30 31 32 33 34 35 36 37 38 39 40 41 42

11 **33** 1 mark

> **Note to parents**
> Some children may simply count on from 24.
> Others may add 10 then subtract 1 as a quick method for adding 9.

12 **Indication of 5 units in the column for milkshake. Colouring of boxes, ticks in boxes or the numbers 1 to 5 written in the boxes are all acceptable.** 1 mark

13 **4** 1 mark

> **Note to parents**
> Using bar charts or graphs is a useful and common way of representing information clearly and concisely. Children can practise constructing them using a variety of data which is easy to collect and they will encounter them in various areas of the curriculum.

14 **Colour any 2 cakes.** 1 mark

> **Note to parents**
> When finding a quarter of a number of objects the child will divide the objects into four groups.
> This can be practised around the home using a variety of objects.

ANSWERS: TEST A

15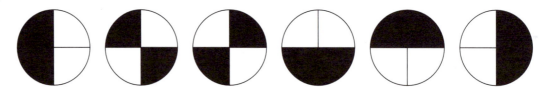

Any one of the examples shown above.   1 mark

Note to parents
Children should be able to recognise simple fractions of a set or of one whole.
In this question there is the opportunity to show that two quarters are equal to one half.
Children can practise cutting objects (such as cakes or apples) into halves and quarters and counting the pieces.

16   Indication is needed here of the **'Majorca'** and **'London'** labels, that is those with only 4 straight sides. No other shapes are allowed. The circles round the shapes are not essential as long as some indication has been clearly made.   1 mark

Note to parents
This question requires the child to read and understand the vocabulary that is associated with shape.

17   **30p, thirty, 30.**   1 mark

Note to parents
Children can benefit greatly from access to counting and using money in both role play and real situations.

18   5 + 4 = **9**   1 mark
     8 + **4** = 12   1 mark
     4 + 11 = 15   1 mark

Note to parents
This question involves some recall of addition facts to 20 and carrying out an inverse operation. Children may find using a number line or counting apparatus useful in order to visualise the problem.

19   **2, 14, 35, 79, 97, 152**.   1 mark
     All numbers, in correct order, must be shown.

ANSWERS: TEST A

> **Note to parents**
> This question is about sequencing numbers and appreciating the place values of digits in numbers; for example, appreciating the difference between 79 and 97. Cards with numbers up to, say, 200 can be made, and your child can arrange them in order.

20 **67** — 1 mark

> **Note to parents**
> Children need to be able to add two digit numbers (i.e. tens and units) which involves exchange, and establish a written technique to do so. They may also have begun to develop mental strategies to do this.
>
> The child may add mentally like this:
>
> e.g. 30 + 20 = 50   or   40 + 30 = 70
>   8 + 9 = 17   (both numbers rounded up to nearest 10
>   50 + 17 = 67   38 rounded to 40 by adding 2
>   29 rounded to 30 by adding 1)
>   1 + 2 = 3
>   70 - 3 = 67
>
> The written technique is generally set out in vertical columns.
>
> T U
> 3 8
> +2 9
> ───
> 6 7
> 1

21 **4, four** — 1 mark

> **Note to parents**
> Children can experience sharing objects (such as sweets or toys) with friends to give equal amounts.

22 **3:55** — 1 mark

> **Note to parents**
> Children need to be able to read digital as well as analogue clocks. Here the child is adding on 15 minutes to the start time and the answer must be in numbers not words.

23 **70** — 1 mark

> **Note to parents**
> This question requires knowledge of the multiples of 10, i.e. 10 × 7 = 70.

ANSWERS: TEST A

24 **56** — 1 mark

> **Note to parents**
> This question involves subtracting one two-digit number from another.
>
> ```
>   T U
>   8 8
> - 3 2
>   ---
>   5 6
> ```
>
> Encourage your child to work out the answer mentally and describe what he or she did, e.g. 'I took 2 units away from 8 which left 6 and I took 3 tens from 8 tens which left 5 tens which is 50. So 50 add 6 is 56'.

25 **Diamond, square, triangle** — 3 marks

Give one mark for each shape correctly identified, no marks for more than three shapes.

> **Note to parents**
> This question is about the reflective symmetry of 2D shapes. If a mirror is placed along the mirror line, the image in the mirror will complete the shape exactly.

26 **30, 90**. — 1 mark

Both answers must be given for mark.

> **Note to parents**
> Children should be able to recognise that any whole number that can be divided exactly by ten will end with a zero.

27 **20p** — 1 mark

> **Note to parents**
> Children need to know that £1.00 is the same as 100p and that there are five twenties in 100.

28 The crayon is **8 cm** long. Accept $7\frac{1}{2}$ cm or $8\frac{1}{2}$ cm. — 1 mark

The pencil is **12 cm** long. Accept $11\frac{1}{2}$ cm or $12\frac{1}{2}$ cm. — 1 mark

> **Note to parents**
> This question involves the accurate use of a ruler that measures in centimetres.

29 The pencil is **4 cm** longer than the crayon. — 1 mark

> **Note to parents**
> The difference in length, i.e. how much longer the pencil is than the crayon, is required.

ANSWERS: TEST A

30 **6 faces** — 1 mark

8 corners — 1 mark

> **Note to parents**
> Handling and recognising 3D objects is encouraged and the ability to transfer 3D experiences to 2D images on paper is required. Children can look for 3D shapes in the environment.

31 **3 faces** — 1 mark

> **Note to parents**
> Making 3D shapes can assist with the child's understanding of how many faces the shapes have. They will see that a cylinder, for example, has two circular faces and the third curved face is actually a rectangle.

32 **£2.50** with the decimal point correctly shown, also accept **£2-50, £2.50p, 2 50** (space between **2** and **50** must be clear), **2 50p,** or any of these in words. — 1 mark

> **Note to parents**
> This requires the child to add up two monetary amounts and represent the answer in a suitable way.

33 4 8 12 **16 20 24** — 1 mark

All three numbers must be given for mark.

> **Note to parents**
> The pattern should be recognised as adding four to the previous number. This is made easier if the child has knowledge of multiplication tables.

34 **19 and 12** *or* **16 and 9** — 1 mark

Only 1 mark is available even if both options are indicated.

> **Note to parents**
> This question requires understanding of the term 'difference' between two numbers, i.e. subtraction.

35 A rectangle or a square may be drawn of any size using the dots as a guide to show right angles. — 1 mark

> **Note to parents**
> A right angle is a 'square corner'. Recognising right angles in 2D shapes is a criterion for sorting them. Children may recognise shapes in their home, or in the street, that have right angles.

ANSWERS: TEST B

TEST B

1 **5** 1 mark

> **Note to parents**
> Knowledge of multiplication tables up to 5 x 5 is required at this level.

2 **10p, 5p, 5p, 2p, 1p** 1 mark

   (All of the above coins must be ringed to gain mark)

> **Note to parents**
> Children should be familiar with coinage up to amounts of 99p.

3 **6** 1 mark

> **Note to parents**
> As in question 1, Test A, mental subtraction and mathematical language are being tested.

4 **3** or **5** or **7** 1 mark

> **Note to parents**
> Recognition of odd numbers is required.

5   1 mark

> **Note to parents**
> Identification of regular solid shapes is needed. Awareness of such shapes in the environment is helpful.

6 **7** and **8** or **6** and **9** 1 mark

7 **6** and **9** or **7** and **8** 1 mark

> **Note to parents**
> Allow one pair of answers for each question. The pairs must be different for the two questions in order to award a mark for each answer.

44

ANSWERS: TEST B

8 32 + 9 = 41   1 mark
42 + 9 = 51   1 mark

Note to parents
Your child should recognise the pattern forming as the numbers are increasing by ten whilst the nine is constant.

9 **35**, 36, **37**, 38, **39**, 40, 41, **42**.   1 mark

Note to parents
This question aims to encourage your child to explore numbers from 1 to 20. It involves ordering numbers in correct sequence, adding on 1, and knowing which number precedes or follows another.

10 **6, 10, 14, 30**.   1 mark

Note to parents
Even numbers are those which form pairs exactly. They will end with the digits 0, 2, 4, 6, 8.

11 **8 cm**, accept $7\frac{1}{2}$ cm or $8\frac{1}{2}$ cm   1 mark

12 A **13 cm** line should be drawn; also accept $12\frac{1}{2}$ cm or $13\frac{1}{2}$ cm   1 mark

Note to parents
Accurate use of a centimetre ruler is required allowing $\frac{1}{2}$ cm each way.

13 **25**   1 mark

Note to parents
Children need to recognise the different ways an addition can be set out.

14 **5p, 1p, 1p, 2p** or **5p, 2p, 2p**.   1 mark

Note to parents
Children will see that there are different ways of making the same amount of money. The coins indicated must add up exactly to 9p.

ANSWERS: TEST B

15 **23, 20, 17, 14, 9, 8, 3.** 1 mark

Note to parents

This question is about sequencing numbers. No marks to be awarded if your child starts with the smallest number, as reading and understanding the mathematical language is important.

16 **Zahid** 1 mark
17 **9** 1 mark
18 **46** 1 mark

Note to parents

At Level 3, children need to extract and interpret information displayed in a bar chart. This is a horizontal bar chart with a scale of one square representing two units.

19 **3 : 40** 1 mark
   Forty minutes past three or **Twenty to four** or **Three forty** 1 mark
20 **4 : 10** or **Ten past four** or **Ten minutes past four** 1 mark

Note to parents

The child is required to match digital to analogue times and express times in words.

21 $\frac{3}{4}$ 1 mark
22 $\frac{1}{3}$ 1 mark

Note to parents

The number of parts a shape is divided into determines the name of the fraction. For example, a shape divided into three has thirds.
A card matching game could be made for reinforcement.

23 **86** 1 mark

Note to parents

Encourage children to reorganise numbers mentally, e.g. 39+47 = 40+46 = 86.

ANSWERS: TEST B

24 **4**   1 mark

> **Note to parents**
> Your child has to find out the difference in the number of children in Class 2 and Class 3 by subtraction or counting on.

25 **38**   1 mark

> **Note to parents**
> This question involves exchange of a ten for units.
>
>   62
> − 24
>   38
>
> Exchange one of the tens from 62 to give 5 tens and 12 units. Then 4 from 12 is 8. Now subtract 2 tens from 5 tens to give 3 tens. Encourage mental calculations, e.g. 62-20 = 42, 42-4 = 38.

26 **6**   1 mark

> **Note to parents**
> To find a quarter of a number of objects, divide them into 4 groups.

27 15, 20, **25**, 30, 35, **40**   1 mark

> **Note to parents**
> This pattern should be recognised as adding 5 each time. This is made easier if the child has knowledge of the multiplication table.

28 20, **30**, **40**, 50, **60**   1 mark

> **Note to parents**
> As in Question 27 a pattern is recognisable. This time each number is increased by 10 and the multiplication table will help.

29 Nearest to 20: **21, 23, 24**   1 mark
     Nearest to 30: **25, 26, 32**   1 mark

> **Note to parents**
> This question involves rounding numbers to the nearest ten. When a number is halfway between (for example, 25), it is generally said to be nearer to the higher ten i.e. 30.

ANSWERS: TEST B

30 **30 minutes** — 1 mark

Note to parents

Your child needs to work out the duration of the journey. He or she will read the start time and then can count round in five minute intervals until the finish time is reached. The numbers of minutes elapsed will then have been counted.

31

1 mark awarded for each line drawn — 2 marks

Note to parents

A mirror can be used to help locate where the lines of symmetry should be drawn.

32 **88 − 69 = 19** — 1 mark

Note to parents

Before finding the difference between various pairs of numbers the child should recognise that 19 is near to 20 and that it is easier to find two numbers which may have a difference near to 20, and try them first.

33 Rectangle and square: — 2 marks

Note to parents

A right angle is a square corner. Children can look for right angles around the home.

34 **Class 4** — 1 mark
    5 — 1 mark
35 **3** — 1 mark

Note to parents

This question requires the child to read information from a table and use it to answer questions.

ANSWERS: TEST C

TEST C

1. a **£1.74** or **1 74p** or **174p** or **£1 74**
   b **£1.45** or **1 45p** or **145p** or **£1 45**
   c **£1.57** or **1 57p** or **157p** or **£1 57** — 3 marks

> **Note to parents**
> This question requires addition of two 2-digit numbers using written or mental computation techniques. If performing a written method the child will find that the answer will be in hundreds, tens and units where the hundreds figure is the pound number.

2. a **17p** b **12p** c **4p** — 3 marks

> **Note to parents**
> This involves subtracting the smaller of the two amounts from the larger to find how much more one child has than another.

3. **44p** — 2 marks

   If your child has only worked out how much Tom spent, i.e. 35p, then award one mark.

> **Note to parents**
> This problem can be approached in a variety of ways. Your child may subtract the price of each item, one at a time, from Tom's original total. Or your child may find the total cost of what Tom bought, and subtract this amount from his total.
> i.e. 23p + (3 x 4p) = 23p + 12p = 35p
> then   79p - 35p = 44p

4. **105, 90, 37, 14, 9, 3** — 1 mark

   All six numbers must be shown in the correct order.

> **Note to parents**
> See Question 15 Test B and Question 19 Test A

5. **258** — 1 mark

> **Note to parents**
> Working this answer out requires careful addition. Watch for careless mistakes when performing an addition of several numbers.

ANSWERS: TEST C

6 There are exactly ten times as many **blue cars** as **motorbikes**. 1 mark

> **Note to parents**
> Children working at Level 4 should be able to recognise that a number ending in zero is a multiple of ten. Their understanding of place value will enable them to see that 90 is ten times 9.

7 **£272.00** or **£272**

> **Note to parents**
> This question involves much calculation and requires the child to approach it in a methodical way, for example:

Total number of cars: 105 + 90 + 37 = 232

Cost for cars:	232 × £1.00 = **£232.00**	1 mark
Cost for vans:	14 × £2.00 = **£28.00**	1 mark
Cost for motorbikes:	9 × 50p = 450p = **£4.50**	1 mark
Cost for coaches:	3 × £2.50 = **£7.50**	1 mark

Total cost   232.00
              28.00
               4.50
           +   7.50
           ─────────
              £272.00   1 mark

8 **262**   1 mark

> **Note to parents**
> Your child needs to be able to perform subtraction involving exchange of hundreds for tens. Encourage your child to use mental strategies for calculating the answer. Practise strategies using different numbers.
>
>   427
> − 165
> ─────
>   262

ANSWERS: TEST C

9   a **17 cm**   b **16 cm**   2 marks

Note to parents

The child should understand that perimeter is the distance all the way round a shape and it must be measured accurately using a centimetre ruler.

10   **2 hours 31 minutes** or **151 minutes** or **2 : 31 hours**.   1 mark

Note to parents

It is important that the child understands that there are 60 minutes in one hour. The child can count how many minutes there are until 5 o'clock i.e. 24 minutes, then how many hours between 5 o'clock and 7 o'clock and finally add the minutes after 7 o'clock.

11   a   **6**   1 mark
    b   **3**   1 mark
    c   **6**   1 mark
    d $\frac{1}{10}$ 1 mark
    e   **6**   dogs
       6   hamsters
       3   cats
       3   fish
       12 no pets   1 mark

Note to parents

40% of the class is equal to 12 children. Therefore, 10% of the class is a quarter of this which is 3 children. An alternative way of working out 10% is this:

$$\frac{10}{100} \times 30 = 3$$

To work out $\frac{1}{5}$, divide 30 by 5 to give 6.
To work out what fraction 3 is of 30, divide 3 by 30 to give $\frac{1}{10}$.

ANSWERS: TEST C

12 Pets owned by children in Class 7B

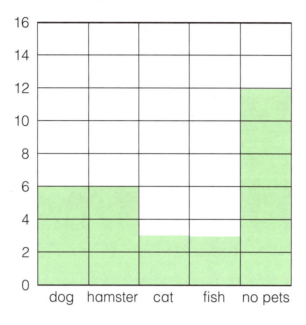

Allow one mark for dog, hamster and no pets correctly shown and 2 marks for cat and fish correctly shown.

3 marks

Note to parents
The scale for number of children is one square representing two units. So an odd number must be shown halfway up the box (see cat or fish). Colouring or shading of the boxes is allowed.

FINDING YOUR CHILD'S LEVEL

Use the marking grids on pages 54 and inside back cover and add up your child's score after each test is attempted. Then refer to the tables below to find the level (and grade if Level 2).

For tests A and B your child will score a number of marks out of a maximum of 41 marks for each test.

If your child scores very highly, i.e. 35 or above for each test, then it may be appropriate to test him or her at Level 4.

By referring to the table, you will be able to identify whether your child has achieved:

- an ungraded result;
- at Level 1;
- at the threshold of Level 2 (graded as 2C);
- in the middle of Level 2 (graded as 2B);
- very well at Level 2 and able to achieve in some areas of Level 3 (graded as 2A);
- at Level 3.

TEST A OR B MARKS

Number of marks	1–4	5–9	10–14	15–20	21–28	28–41
Level	Ungraded	Level 1	Level 2C achieved	Level 2B achieved	Level 2A achieved	Level 3 achieved

TEST C MARKS

Number of marks	20 or below	21–28
Level	Working towards Level 4	At Level 4

MARKING

HOW TO MARK THE QUESTIONS

When marking your child's test it is important to remember that the answers given are sample answers. You must look carefully at your child's answers, and the 'Notes to parents' with the sample answers, and judge whether they deserve credit. Award the mark if the answer deserves credit.

At the end of Key Stage 1 your child's spelling may show a number of errors. Do not mark any answer wrong because the words are misspelt. Read the word aloud and if it sounds correct, award the mark.

When you go through the tests with your child, try to be positive. Look for the good things that have been done, in addition to showing where errors have been made.

Enter your child's marks onto the chart and then refer to the levelling chart in the answer section of this book.

MARKING GRIDS

TEST A

Question	Marks available	Marks scored	Question	Marks available	Marks scored
1	1		19	1	
2	1		20	1	
3	1		21	1	
4	1		22	1	
5	1		23	1	
6	1		24	1	
7	1		25	3	
8	1		26	1	
9	1		27	1	
10	1		28	2	
11	1		29	1	
12	1		30	2	
13	1		31	1	
14	1		32	1	
15	1		33	1	
16	1		34	1	
17	1		35	1	
18	3		Total	41	